SUPERBASE 15
NAVY JAX

SUPERBASE 15

NAVY JAX

Sub-Hunters and Light Strikers

George Hall

Published in 1990 by Osprey Publishing
Limited
59 Grosvenor Street, London W1X 9DA

British Library Cataloguing in Publication
Data
Superbase navy Jax. – (Superbase).
  1. United States. Air bases
  I. Hall, George, *1941*– II. Series
358.4′17′0973

ISBN 0–84045–976–1

Editor Tony Holmes
Designed by Paul Kime
Printed in Hong Kong

Front cover Fully bombed up and
raring to go, a VA-46 'Clansmen'
A-7E Corsair sits on the steamy NAS
Cecil Field ramp awaiting its pilot.
Other squadron aircraft in various
stages of arming can be seen beneath
the SLUF's port wing. In the distance
the Hornet's 'nest' is slowly
encroaching upon the Corsair's ramp
space

Back cover A trainee Seahawk pilot
slowly winds on the power as his
sleek mount climbs away from NAS
Mayport. A formidable weapons
package, the SH-60B is a vital spear in
the US Navy's anti-submarine warfare
arsenal

Title pages Basking in the warm
Florida sunshine, a trio of 'Clansmen'
from VA-46 complete their preflight
checks before engine spool-up and
take off. The various black leads
trailing away from each Corsair are
linked to a below hardstand power
outlet, thus allowing the pilots to
check their instrumentation and
various on board 'black boxes'
before the aircraft is actually running

Photo notes: As with all
SUPERBASE books to date, the
author uses Nikon cameras,
primarily the superb new F-4
model, and a variety of Nikkor
lenses ranging from 15 mm to
500 mm. The film, with very few
exceptions, is Kodachrome 64.

Right Being a true naval facility,
where would NAS Cecil Field be
without its ship's bell, anchors and
chain. As with everything Navy, the
brass is kept gleaming and the paint
is maintained in spotless condition

For a catalogue of all books published by Osprey Aerospace
please write to:

**The Marketing Manager, Consumer Catalogue Department
Osprey Publishing Ltd, 59 Grosvenor Street, London, W1X 9DA**

Introduction

Located on the Atlantic coast of northern Florida, the city of Jacksonville has served America's airborne, surface, and undersea navies since the turn of the century. To the Navy or Marine Corps pilot, NAVY JAX refers to three separate bases within the city of Jacksonville: NAS Jacksonville, NAS Cecil Field, and NAS Mayport. Each base caters to an entirely unique aspect of modern naval aviation.

NAS Jacksonville has hosted naval aviators since the mid-1930s. It was a huge pilot training centre during World War 2, when it was also utilized as a POW camp for some 2000 German prisoners. The base was the first home of the Blue Angels; the flight demonstration team gave its first public show near the base in 1946.

The shift in emphasis towards anti-submarine warfare took place at NAS Jacksonville in the 1950s. Today it is one of the Navy's biggest VP bases, hosting several squadrons of P-3C Orions and SH-3 anti-sub helicopters. NAS Jacksonville is also the principal base for naval aviation's in-house airline; the 'VRs' in their C-9 Skytrain IIs, crewed primarily by naval reservists, are seen on the main runway at all hours.

The other main activity at NAS Jacksonville is the gigantic Naval Aviation Depot, a facility for modifying and overhauling most types of naval aircraft.

Some eight miles to the north-west is NAS Cecil Field, a 21,000-acre facility that is the Navy's largest master jet base in the United States. Cecil is fighter and attack country, home to the east coast RAG (Replacement Air Group) for the F/A-18 Hornet strike fighter and, for a while longer, a collection of ageing but still capable A-7 Corsair II attack aircraft. The four A-7 squadrons still at Cecil expect to have transitioned to the vastly more capable Hornet by the end of 1991.

One other modern Navy jet hums around the pattern at Cecil—the S-3 Viking, a portly but handsome twin-jet that provides long-range anti-submarine protection for the carrier battle group.

The much-improved S-3B model is now operational out of Cecil, with much more powerful electronics systems for sorting undersea targets and with the added capability of slinging Harpoon anti-ship missiles under its wings.

Back on the Atlantic shore is NAS Mayport, a small base dedicated exclusively to the operation of the SH-60 Seahawk helicopter. This excellent platform, a navalized derivative of Sikorsky's Black Hawk troop-carrier, is used as a close-in anti-submarine defender, operating from a variety of surface warships. Mayport lies adjacent to a collection of docks for naval surface ships, including the two super carriers, *Saratoga* (CV-60), and *Forrestal* (CV-59).

NAVY JAX also gives a nod to another long-time fixture of the local aviation community, the Florida Air National Guard. The state's only flying Guard unit performs an air-defence mission out of the commercial airport north of town, mounted aboard the hard-to-beat F-16 Falcon. This highly experienced fighter unit, loaded with multi-thousand-hour Air Force fighter 'jocks', is everyone's favourite dogfighting adversary in the south-east US. The guard bums sally forth daily to manhandle the Cecil Hornets, the Marine Corps F/A-18 drivers out of Beaufort, South Carolina, and the Air Force students learning the intricacies of the F-15 Eagle over at Tyndall AFB on Florida's Gulf of Mexico shore.

Let's jump in the Hertzmobile and cover the bases; be assured of heavy flight ops from dawn to midnight at each location. As with virtually all American air bases, access is stringently restricted; don't show up at the main gate and expect a day of photo opportunities. We were enthusiastically and knowledgeably escorted by several public affairs professionals including Bert Byers, Paul Henkemeyer, Veronica Schauer, and Joe Sarver at the Naval Aviation Depot. Their help in telling the story of NAVY JAX is greatly appreciated.

Contents

Painted up as a VA-46 machine, this particular airframe, BuNo 152650, was actually the seventh A-7A constructed, and the very first Corsair ever to touch down on a carrier. This momentous event took place on 14 November 1966 when Lt Cdr Fred Hueber of the Naval Air Test Center caught the wire on the angled steel of USS *America* (CV-66) while the vessel sailed along the coast near Norfolk, Virginia. The majority of the type's carrier qualification trials were carried out by this aircraft during late 1966 and early 1967

A dwindling breed

Right The plane-captain signals to his pilot that the Allison TF-41 turbofan has successfully ignited. Soon the power starter connector seen trailing away from the rear of the Corsair will be removed and safely stored, the maintenance doors flanking either side of the fuselage will be securely fastened shut and the pilot will unfold the aircraft's wings and prepare to taxi out. The plane-captain performs a vital function during the critical moments of start up as the pilot has little visibility over his shoulders, and needs to keep his eyes intently planted on his instrument panel just in case something malfunctions. Mounted on the stores pylons are Mk 82 500 lb retarded bombs, whilst the inner station has an LTV Forward Looking Infra-red (FLIR) pod firmly attached to it

Below The nose gear is fully extended, the leading edge slats drooped and the all-moving tailplane is angled sharply down. In a matter of milli-seconds 'Clansman' 311 will be unstuck from the Cecil runway and clawing its way into the powdery blue Florida sky. The lack of stores on the aircraft indicate that the pilot could be taking this veteran A-7E up for a proving flight after a period of maintenance, or perhaps he just wants to increase his hours on a type that won't be around for much longer

Blast off! Same aircraft, different squadron. A rather weather beaten Corsair from VA-72 'Blue Hawks' leaves Cecil behind in a shimmering heat haze. The ejector racks mounted beneath each wing carry a couple of small 25 lb blue practice bombs. The 'Blue Hawks' began life as a fighter squadron before being redesignated into the growing attack community in 1955. They traded in their battle weary F9F-2 Panthers the following year for brand new A-4A Skyhawks, thus becoming the first squadron in the Navy to become operational on 'Heineman's Hot Rod'. VA-72 moved to NAS Cecil Field from Oceana, Virginia, in 1965 following their first combat cruise to Vietnam. They returned to South-east Asia the following year aboard USS *Franklin D Roosevelt* (CVA-42), but this was to be their last war cruise. In September 1969 the 'Blue Hawks' finally said goodbye to their faithful A-4s and reformed on the A-7B Corsair, the more powerful Echo model eventually being phased in during the mid 1970s. Along with the 'Clansmen', VA-72 are the last frontline A-7E unit at NAS Cecil Field, the squadron due to transition onto the F/A-18 Hornet in the very near future. The white mass in the hazy distance just in front of the A-7 is a P-3 Orion from NAS Jacksonville, which is 'shooting' touch and goes on Cecil's main runway

Above Although the low viz sword beneath the cockpit says otherwise, the man with his bottom strapped to this particular Corsair is none other than Commander 'Fast Eddy' Fahy, the head 'Clansman'. As with all other air wing squadrons, the CO's machine in VA-46 is 01, the 'double nuts' (00) modex reserved exclusively for the Commander Air Group (CAG)

Left 'Fast Eddy' confers with his plane-captain soon after strapping into 'Clansman' 300. Besides the retarded Mk 82s and the almost mandatory FLIR pod, the CO's A-7 is also adorned with a practice AIM-9L Sidewinder, just in case the adversary boys from VF-45 'Blackbirds' decide to get in his way. The Corsair lacks the thrust to weight ratio of the emaciated A-4F so it's a 'throttles to the gate' situation should an 'enemy' appear

Left It's rather warm in the cockpit of a stationary Corsair during summertime in Florida, especially if you're ensconced in a bone dome and flight suit. Sleeves rolled up and arms resting on the canopy rails, the pilot waits for the preflight checks to be completed. Besides the refuelling probe which is clearly visible in the extended position, the auxiliary power ram-air generator is also deployed, the small propellor driven pod being situated within the fuselage alongside the FLIR

Above The sturdiness of the wing pylons is emphasized in this close-up view of a fully armed A-7E. The FLIR pod attached to this Corsair relies heavily on the aircraft's inertial navigation system, but more than doubles the bomb delivery accuracy of a pilot during night attacks. The pod is controlled through the Navigation/Weapons Delivery System (NWDS) computer, and it may be used on all current attack modes flown by Corsair squadrons

Opposite above The old and the very new. A weary 'Clansmen' A-7E taxies past two brand new Charlie model Hornets of VFA-136 'Knighthawks' as they refuel at the hot pad after a sortie. Long term members of Air Wing Seven, VA-46, along with sister squadron VA-72, transferred to Air Wing Three during 1989 in preparation for a Mediterranean cruise on board USS *John F Kennedy* (CV-67)

Opposite below Soon the only Corsairs regularly flying at Cecil will all belong to this outfit, the 'Blue Dolphins' of VA-203, one of three Naval Reserve squadrons equipped with the A-7E. The splash of blue on the tail actually represents the map of Florida. An integral part of CVWR-20, the 'Dolphins' formed up in July 1970 and were initially based at nearby NAS Jacksonville. As with most light attack squadrons they cut their teeth on the Skyhawk before transitioning onto the A-7B, and then finally to the A-7E in the mid-1980s when frontline units began receiving the Hornet

Above Now this is 'Fast Eddy' Fahy's Corsair! However, that's not the man in the driver's seat. The 'Clansmen' have the distinction of being the first jet attack squadron commissioned into the Navy, this lofty honour being bestowed upon them on 1 July 1955 at NAS Cecil Field. Initially equipped with the sexy F9F-8 Cougar, they soon transitioned onto the A-4B Skyhawk. Many Med cruises on several carriers punctuated the next decade, before the 'Clansmen' joined CVW-17 aboard USS *Forrestal* (CV-59) for their baptism of fire over Vietnam. Back at Cecil in 1968, VA-46 finally got to daub their distinctive tartan colours upon the new A-7B Corsair. Eventually VA-46 received the ultimate Corsair, the Echo model, and has flown this type ever since

Although the A-7 is currently enjoying the twilight of its long career, regular extensive maintenance and reworking of airframes is still being carried out at Cecil Field. Here the dreaded Tactical Paint Scheme (TPS) comes in for a battering as a suitably clothed technician liberally douses the fuselage in paint stripper. All the vulnerable areas like the canopy, radome and undercarriage assemblies have been securely masked off before the stripping process is begun. The chin mounted General Electric M61A-1 Vulcan is also missing from this airframe, as is the Allison powerplant

19

The new light-attacker

Drifting over the ramp towards the runway, 'Gladiator' 343 nears the end of another training sortie. This Hornet is a perfect example of the current spec of F/A-18 leaving the factory at St Louis, BuNo 163474 having all the mods associated with the C/D model airframes now entering Navy service. Starting from the nose and working aft, the small white blisters just forward of the modex, and atop the spine, house new AN/ALQ-65 airborne self-protection jammers which can be alternated with the Sanders AN/ALQ-126B system already fitted to the Alpha model Hornets. Bolted to the leading edge extensions (LEXs) are the now familiar 'wedges', devices which McDonnell Douglas believe will finally cure the buffet stress which has for so long afflicted the elegant twin tails of the Hornet. A close look at the base of the starboard vertical surface reveals another measure taken by the factory to solve the stress problem, the fitting of three strengthened bolts to stiffen the anchor point of the tail to the fuselage. This rather nondescript F/A-18D belongs to VFA-106 'Gladiators', the east coast Replacement Air Group (RAG) squadron for light attack units

Right Not exactly a combat formation, but it certainly makes for a mouth watering photograph. High above the tranquil mid Atlantic, a close grouping of Hornet 'jocks' prove that when it comes to fancy flying nobody does it better than Navy light attack

Above All is quiet on the ramp at the end of another day's flying. Work continues on after dark as this is about the only time the majority of squadron aircraft are shutdown on the ground. The full span drooping ailerons and inboard single slotted Fowler flaps are clearly visible in this silhouette shot, as are the rear vision mirrors mounted to the canopy frame

Left As the 'groundie' secures an access panel near the radar jammer blisters, the trainee Hornet driver carefully climbs aboard his new steed. The integral ladder fits snugly into the undersurface LEX, thus averting the problem of cumbersome ground equipment littering the pan, or the already overcrowded flightdeck. A trainee pilot arrives at the RAG after completing his two years of basic flying at one of several training stations spread throughout Texas and Florida. He will then spend roughly six months with VFA-106 learning everything there is to know about the Hornet, before being posted to an operational unit. The 'Gladiators' have about 30 aircraft on strength, operating a mixed fleet of Alpha, Bravo, Charlie and Delta model Hornets

Below Briefly caught by a shaft of sunlight breaking through the heavy murk above, a pair of lightly armed Hornets taxi out to the holding point before departing as a pair for an ACM sortie (*Courtesy Tony Holmes*)

Left While a Hornet lines up to shoot yet another touch and go at Cecil, a 'Knighthawk' glances across at a squadron mate parked alongside him. Mounted to the outboard stores pylon is a triple ejector rack (TER), lightly loaded with six 25 lb blue bombs. Like VFA-137, the 'Knighthawks' have only been part of naval aviation for a handful of years, but unlike the 'Kestrels', who stood up at Cecil, VFA-136 was initially activated on the other side of the country at NAS Lemoore, home of light strike on the west coast (*Courtesy Tony Holmes*)

Above Although the aircraft may look like a scrap merchant's dream, it does in fact belong to a squadron who currently hold the Battle Efficiency 'E', plus the Maintenance 'M' for east coast Hornet units, as the two stylized letters near the nose denote. The 'Kestrels' are a relatively new squadron having only stood up with the Hornet for the first time in July 1985. VFA-137 has been attached to CVW-13 since that time, and has participated with fellow Hornet squadrons VFA-131 and 136 on several Med cruises aboard the venerable *Coral Sea* (CV-43) (*Courtesy Tony Holmes*)

Proving that Hornets do occasionally wear something other than grey, the CO's F/A-18B is a virtual riot of colour compared to its squadron compatriots. The unit citations on the spine have been awarded to VFA-106 for churning out quality naval aviators year after year. This particular Hornet was one of the last B models to leave the St Louis plant (*Courtesy Tony Holmes*)

Above While the instructor braces himself for take-off, the student pilot gently eases the throttle levers forward before releasing the brake and spearing down the runway. The excellent field of vision afforded to the backseat occupant is clearly visible from this angle. Unfortunately for devotees of squadron markings, 'Gladiator' 356 is fairly typical of the unit's less than inspiring colours

Left Owned by the oldest east coast Hornet squadron, a 'markingless' Hornet crackles down the black top in full military power. The 'Wildcats' of VFA-131 were formally established at NAS Lemoore on 3 October 1983, the unit staying on the west coast until February 1985 when they transitted across the continent to Cecil. Attached to the predominantly Hornet equipped CVW-13 aboard *Coral Sea* (CV-43) for four years, the 'Wildcats' recently replaced VA-46 and VA-72 within Air Wing Seven, and they now call the much larger deck of USS *Eisenhower* (CVN-69) home

Left The murky cloud below provides the perfect backdrop for this pair of drab grey 'Golden Hawks'. The Naval Reserve is currently updating all of its equipment to bring it more into line with frontline air wings. Manning these aircraft is one problem the Reserve does not share with the full time Navy, most squadrons having an abundance of experienced crews

Below One squadron not too often spied in the skies above Cecil is Lemoore based VFA-303 'Golden Hawks', one of two reserve Hornet units in the US Navy. Attached to CVWR-30, the 'Golden Hawks' recently completed their first shipboard deployment aboard USS *Enterprise* (CVN-65) and are now fully operational after experiencing an extended transitional period. During the two week cruise they, and sister squadron VFA-307, set an amazing record of 68 landings in 60 minutes, an average interval of 48 seconds between aircraft crossing the ramp being maintained for precisely an hour. This early production Hornet is carrying a telemetry pod beneath the starboard wing and an active seeker AIM-9L Sidewinder round on the port wing railings. As was the case on most early F/A-18s, this Hornet wears the interim medium grey/powder grey scheme initially applied to Navy machines by McDonnell Douglas

Right A remarkable self-portrait of a 'Golden Hawk' and two of his squadron mates. The sheer bulkiness of the pilot's survival vest, G-suit and oxygen mask make this photo even more impressive because there is not a lot of room to manoeuvre in the Hornet's cockpit with the joystick in one hand and a Nikon in the other

Below Shock waves ripple back over the twin tails as a Hornet driver puts his clean mount through its paces in the clear blue Florida skies. The compactness of the aircraft's underfuselage can be appreciated from this angle, a neatness due in no small part to the overall size of the F/A-18's powerplants: two General Electric F404-GE-400 turbofans. 'Bat turns' are a speciality of Hornet pilots the world over, and it is a manoeuvre perhaps matched only in the west by the F-16 Fighting Falcon

Above The 'Gladiators' also operate a large fleet of single seaters alongside the two place F/A-18 B/Ds. A detachment of six to eight aircraft and supporting personnel is maintained at NAS Fallon, Nevada, for much of the year to provide weapons delivery training for new Hornet pilots. During the six months of his course, a new pilot will visit Fallon twice, both times for a period of about 14 days. In fact, the culmination of his training is an intensive two weeks of fighting the 'Bandits' and 'Cylons' of VF-126 and VFA-127, and then delivering his weapons on target, avoiding simulated SAMs and triple-AAA along the way. Posting to a frontline squadron after this little test is considered to be a well earned rest for the pilots concerned!

Right NAS Cecil Field is one of four Master Jet Bases in the US Navy, and a quick glance at its flightline at any time of the day will soon confirm why. Besides the 33 Hornets visible in this panoramic view of the light attack pan, 11 A-7Es, two visiting F-14s, an E-2C and a solitary low viz EA-6B Prowler complete the picture. Sixteen light attack squadrons are based at Cecil, making this facility an important cog in the overall mechanism that is naval aviation

Above As soon as a mission is completed the pilot taxies his aircraft across to the hot pad and immediately gets his tanks refilled. This allows down time between sorties to be kept to a minimum. This new F/A-18C carries a 330 US gallon drop tank on the centreline station, the standard arrangement seen on virtually all Hornets both on shore and at sea

Right The hot pads have only been operational with the Navy for about two years but all reports indicate they are proving extremely beneficial to both air and groundcrews alike. The recipient of the JP-5 in this instance is an F/A-18D of VFA-106. Between them, the Navy and Marine Corps have over 100 two seaters and they are amongst the hardest worked aircraft in naval aviation. At present only the 'Gladiators', VFA-125 'Rough Raiders' and the 'Sharpshooters' of VMFAT-101 operate the 'twin tub' Hornet. As can be seen, Cecil is actually carved out of the thick vegetation which seems to cover virtually all of Florida (*Courtesy Tony Holmes*)

Above One of the newest members of the Hornet community is VFA-82 'Marauders', a unit that flew the Corsair for 21 years. Along with a change in aircraft came a change in air wings, VFA-82 moving from CVW-8 to CVW-1, the latter having over 50 years experience in carrier aviation. Now sailing aboard the *America* (CV-66), this particular F/A-18C proudly wears a decal of the Air Wing's badge on its tail, the motto beneath the motif reading 'first and foremost'. Only the CAG's mount wore this highly colourful badge, and only his aircraft had the carrier designation latters sprayed on in 'Marauders' blue (*Courtesy Tony Holmes*)

Left Currently, the Marine Corps has no training squadron for Hornet pilots on the east coast so, as this aircraft denotes, VFA-106 is charged with this responsibility as well. A considerable number of 'flying leathernecks' pass through the RAG at Cecil as no less than six Hornet squadrons are based at nearby MCAS Beaufort, South Carolina

The high tech office of the Hornet is dominated by three cathode ray tube (CRT) displays which tell the pilot everything he needs to know about his mount. Technically called Digital Display Indicators (DDIs), they can be clearly seen in this luminous photo; the screen on the left describing the aircraft's current weapons fit; the lower screen presenting navigational information, plus an Horizontal Situation Indicator (HSI); and the DDI on the right indicates to the pilot what his nose mounted Hughes AN/APG-65 radar is seeing. The majority of this information is repeated on his head-up display (HUD)

Above Hornet's don't come much fresher than these five parked side by side on the gloomy Cecil ramp. Their total flying time would probably be a figure less than 300 hours. Having only just completed their transition training onto the aircraft, VFA-81 'Sunliners' managed to steer clear of the air wing shuffle which seemed to plague light attack squadrons in 1988. Wearing the double AA on the inside of their twin fins, the 'Sunliners' have stayed firmly attached to CVW-17, an air wing they have been associated with for many years. As with many east coast VFA units, the 'Sunliners' have added a welcome splash of colour to their CAG aircraft (*Courtesy Tony Holmes*)

Right More representative of the colours worn by Hornet squadrons is this well used reserve machine from VFA-303. Armed with AIM-9L Sidewinders on each wingtip, a reservist is given the last minute 'gouge' from his plane-captain as he goes about strapping himself into the Hornet

Parked outside their own hangar complex, a smart line up of 'Marauders' repose on a Friday afternoon safe in the knowledge that the week's flying is over. Along with the extra ECM blisters on the nose of the Charlie model Hornet, a large white protuberance has also appeared on the forward undercarriage bay door. The gentle shading of the TPS greys on these machines is very noteworthy because after a month of operations this 'perfect blend' will be but a memory for the VFA-82 paint shop to reminisce about (*Courtesy Tony Holmes*)

A gloomy 'Maurauder' waits for the heavens to open up and drown it in steamy rain. Originally a World War 2 fighter squadron, the modern VFA-82 was originally reformed in May 1967 as a VA unit equipped with the then new A-7A Corsair. Over the next four years the 'Marauders' earned their battle spurs over North Vietnam, three deployments taking place in that time. The squadron briefly transitioned onto the A-7E before serious engine problems with the type forced VA-82 back to the A-7C, this version being an Echo model Corsair with the earlier TF30 powerplant. Eventually the top of the range Corsair appeared in 1974 and the 'Maurauders' successfully operated this type up until early 1988 (*Courtesy Tony Holmes*)

Above A 'clipped Kestrel' is towed away to the squadron maintenance hangar for a routine inspection. Birds of prey seem to be popular symbols for VFA squadrons in the US Navy (*Courtesy Tony Holmes*)

Right An aircraft with some considerable history attached to it, BuNo 160781 is the 'granddaddy' of all F/A-18Bs. One of two 'twin tub' Hornets built within the initial batch of 11 F/A-18 prototypes ordered from McDonnell Douglas, this aircraft has performed sterling work for the Naval Air Test Center at NAS Patuxent River. Being off-loaded at NAS Mayport, the aircraft is on its way to the rework facility at Cecil

Cecil scooter

Oh for the days when pilots wore international orange flight suits and flew aircraft with white bellies! Harking back to the early glory days of VA-106, this immaculate A-4C Skyhawk began life in the early 1960s as an A4D-3. Painted up to represent a 'Gladiator' embarked on the beautifully named USS *Shangri-La* (CVA-38) in 1961, this aircraft is soon to be displayed on the gate at Cecil. It is perhaps appropriate at this point to let your imagination wander and think of VFA-106's ramp cluttered with Hornets painted up in light gull grey and glossy insignia white, sky blue Roman bone domes emblazoned on the twin tails. Oh well, we can all dream

Left Back to reality, well almost. At least these 'Super Fox' A-4Fs are glossy. Belonging to Naval Reserve squadron VFC-12 'Fighting Omars', these uniquely painted machines are on one of their periodic detachments from home base, NAS Oceana, Virginia. During the course of 1988 the 'Omars' went on 26 detachments from Oceana, totalling 190 days away from Virginia. Nicknamed 'Home of the Road Gang', the squadron has 35 Reservist officers on strength, the majority of them having an adversary instructor background with about 3500 fast jet hours, 1500 of these on the A-4 alone. Whilst at Cecil, the 'Omars' usually operate closely with VFA-106 and other fleet Hornet and Corsair units. A total of 14 Skyhawks are on strength with the majority of these being single seaters

Above As with most Skyhawk equipped adversary units, VFC-12 relies heavily on the venerable TA-4J. Used to simulate first generation enemy aircraft, the rather underpowered TA-4 is still a tough street fighter when it comes to low speed, low energy air to air combat

Above Another sortie completed, a 'Fighting Omar' makes a smoky recovery at Cecil. In this clean configuration, the Pratt & Whitney J52-P-408 powered A-4F 'Super Fox' is more than a handful for an experienced Hornet 'jock', let alone a 'greenhorn' from VFA-106. The highly polished engine grey scheme worn by VFC-12 is unique to this outfit, and extremely smart to boot

Opposite above Once based at Cecil Field, a stripey 'Blackbird' from VF-45 gently eases down towards the black top. Now 'home ported' in the sunny climes of Key West, the Blackbirds operate a mixed fleet of TA-4s, A-4Es, F-5Es, F-16Ns and TF-16Ns up and down the east coast of the USA. These rather potent machines contrast markedly with the unit's initial equipment, the vibrating MACK truck of the skies, the A-1 Skyraider. Serving for four years as the east coast A-1 RAG, VA-45 eventually received the Skyhawk and began flying dissimilar air combat training (DACT) with it in 1976. Redesignated VF-45 in 1985, the squadron was responsible for developing and implementing the first strike-fighter ACM readiness programme (SFARP) for the F/A-18 in 1986, a programme which keeps the 'Blackbirds' visible in the skies above Jacksonville

Opposite below The only permanently based Skyhawk outfit at Cecil are the 'Flying Gators' of VMA-142, a Marine Corps Reserve unit attached to the 4th Marine Air Wing. This suitably warlike mural graces the hangar wall outside 'Gator Country' (*Courtesy Tony Holmes*)

Although not based at Cecil, the 0A-4Ms of Headquarters and Maintenance Squadron (H&MS-32) regularly deploy south from their base at MCAS Cherry Point to provide forward air control (FAC) for VMA-142, and any other squadron that can use their unique talents. Packed with the A-4M's avionics and radio transmitting equipment, the 'FastFAC' Skyhawk provides the vital link between air and ground forces. The LAU-10A Zuni rocket pod beneath the port wing is used by the pilot to mark the target for incoming aircraft. On the outer pylon on the starboard wing a small triple ejector rack carries several practice bombs. This particular Skyhawk began life as a TA-4F before being upgraded to the more venomous 0A-4M standard in 1979

Above The 'Gators' also fly several two seat TA-4Js alongside the Mike model Skyhawks. Banking around tightly above the TA-4 is a Marine Corps A-6E Intruder on a cross-country from Cherry Point. VMA-142 is one of five reserve squadrons equipped with the Skyhawk, the majority of them now flying the A-4M after operating various models over the past decade. The new found abundance of surplus Mike model Skyhawks stems from frontline squadrons re-equipping with the AV-8B Harrier II (*Courtesy Tony Holmes*)

Right All boarded up against the elements, this weather-beaten A-4M sits silently on the ramp. VMA-142 only transitioned from the Foxtrot to the Mike model Skyhawk in 1988, a transition which was not altogether without its problems. The advanced weapons delivery electronics fitted into the A-4M far surpassed anything previously seen by the 'Gators' and this initially led to some reliability problems. However, the 'groundies' persevered and by the end of 1988 the squadron was again up to strength. The majority of the offending equipment can be seen in this head on shot. The glass sight houses the seeker head for the Hughes Angle Rating Bombing System (ARBS), the cream coloured blisters contain ECM recording and suppression aerials, whilst the bulbous canoe fairing beneath the nose is filled with the APN-153(V) navigation radar (*Courtesy Tony Holmes*)

The Nordic Warrior

Right The other major occupants of Cecil Field control these pugnacious sub-busters. Air Antisubmarine Wing One (VS Wing One) controls six frontline Lockheed Viking squadrons, and the S-3 RAG. Displaying four different types of camouflage, all of these machines belong to one unit, the 'Seawolves' of VS-27

Below The co-pilot's helmet is graphically picked out by the strong afternoon sun as he carefully guides the Viking down towards the Cecil strip. The sturdy undercarriage on the portly S-3 is a direct development from that slung under the classic F-8 Crusader, although the landing habits of the Lockheed product are far more civil than the Vought fighter's ever were

Above Waiting for the 'Hoovers' to spool up, a rather crudely camouflaged S-3A of VS-27 prepares to depart on a training sortie. The podded General Electric TF34 turbofans make a rather strange burping noise when the throttles are opened, and on a recovery approach to a carrier it has to be heard to be believed. Currently transitioning onto the new S-3B Viking, VS-27 recently operated two of the Bravo model aircraft from USS *Forrestal* (CV-59), giving the type its carrier debut. The major modifications to the Viking concern its ASW and anti-shipping capability, Lockheed developing a special package for the Navy and labelling it the weapons system improvement programme (WSIP). Basically this consists of increased acoustic processing capacity, a new sonobuoy telemetry receiver system, expanded ESM capability, better radar processing and compatibility with the deadly Harpoon anti-shipping missile (*Courtesy Tony Holmes*)

Right The VS community is perhaps the most confused of all air wing members when it comes to adopting a standard colour scheme for their S-3s. Some aircraft are still painted up in full pre-TPS colours, as the tail of this VS-31 'Top Cats' Viking illustrates, while others have just had the insignia white removed from their undersides and all corresponding markings toned down to suit. Finally, more and more Vikings are appearing in the fully blown low viz TPS greys. This close up view of 'Top Cat' 701's tail shows the MAD (magnetic anomaly detector) boom stored away between the horizontal tailplanes (*Courtesy Tony Holmes*)

Left Just to confuse matters further not all the spares held at Cecil have been resprayed in TPS! A predominantly low viz S-3A of VS-30 'Diamondcutters' taxies out past several other Vikings towards the runway. Once an extremely colourful squadron, VS-30 liberally daubed the rudders of their Vikings with blood red paint and insignia white diamonds. Now, a plain white radome is the highlight of this particular machine. Attached to CVW-17, the 'Diamondcutters' usually deploy aboard USS *Saratoga* (CV-60). VS-30 is currently transitioning onto the S-3B, thus giving them the distinction of being the first fleet squadron in the US Navy to operate this type (*Courtesy Tony Holmes*)

Below A long term ASW squadron, VS-31 once flew the rattling S-2 Tracker from carrier decks in the 1950s and 60s. Equipped with the Viking since the early 1970s, the 'Top Cats' regularly deploy with the Third and Sixth Fleets aboard USS *Dwight D Eisenhower* (CVN-69). VS-31 seems to be the last VS Squadron on the east coast to still retain colourful markings, although by the look of 'Top Cat' 707 it could soon be in the maintenance shop undergoing a full overhaul and respray (*Courtesy Tony Holmes*)

Above One unit vital to the continued advancement of ASW techniques within the US Navy is the Force Warfare Aircraft Test Directorate, based at NAS Patuxent River, Maryland. Responsible for the overall testing and evaluation of all aspects of ASW equipment and aircraft amongst other things, FORCE operate both S-3A and B model Vikings, and P-3 Orions. This drab S-3A, wearing the FORCE symbol on its tall tail, was briefly deployed to Florida to work with VS-27 on the new avionics systems fitted to the S-3B. During its travels, this particular Viking has picked up a drop tank from VA-97 'Warhawks', quite a unique acquisition when you consider that the 'Warhawks', an A-7E unit, are based at NAS Lemoore, California (*Courtesy Tony Holmes*)

Left A rather battered 'Top Cat' heads seaward in search of Soviet submarines. This particular Viking is the personal mount of VS-31's CO (*Courtesy Tony Holmes*)

Opposite The 'Seawolves' of VS-27. The Viking is an extremely capable ASW platform, but one which operates with a crew of only four. As with all other RAG squadrons, VS-27 is stocked with experienced crews who can impart their frontline fleet techniques to new recruits

Shielding itself from the scorching afternoon sun, a glassy grey 'Seawolf' awaits its next sortie. Although the Viking is a large aircraft, Lockheed built in some rather handy devices to allow a modern carrier to safely operate ten S-3s on a daily basis. Virtually everything that 'sticks out' on the S-3 folds in some way, the high-aspect ratio wing, designed and manufactured by LTV (Vought), halving in size soon after recovering on a carrier deck. The tall slab tail, a prominent feature of the Viking, also folds away flat, allowing VS green shirts to strike the aircraft down to the hangar deck and perform routine maintenance sheltered from the elements

Vikings don't get much patchier than 'Seawolf' 722 seen departing the VS ramp on a training sortie. The Viking crews from Cecil regularly work with P-3 Orions from nearby NAS Jacksonville. When you consider the number of ASW aircraft based in this small area of Florida, woe betide any snooping Soviet submarine commander who fancies chancing his arm in the waters off the east coast of America

Left While the 'groundies' rush around checking the moveable surfaces on this soon to depart S-3, the plane-captain stands out in front keeping the crew informed of what's going on. Correct signalling between the ramp and the cockpit is vital during preflight (*Courtesy Tony Holmes*)

Above Compared to 'Seawolf' 722 this fellow VS-27 S-3 is in showroom condition. Crew entry to the Viking is via the small hatch visible just in front of the engine. Although it is a physically large aircraft, space is at a premium inside, as most of the fuselage is filled with ASW related processors, computers and tactical radar systems

Illustrating perfectly the state of flux the ASW community is currently in, a high viz/low viz Viking taxies into the early morning sun on the Cecil ramp. Wearing the distinctive badge of VS-32 above the modex, the 'Maulers' are attached to Air Wing One and provide the ASW capability for USS *America* (CV-66) and her supporting battlegroup (*Courtesy Tony Holmes*)

Base oddities

Not all aircraft at Cecil are navy grey. Several times a year the Marine Corps invade the base from MCAS New River, North Carolina, to conduct rigorous airborne assault exercises in the swamplands of Florida. These lavishly decorated CH-46Es belong to HMM-162, whilst the lone UH-1N at the end of the line is an HML/A-167 machine. All part of the 2nd Marine Aircraft Wing, the various rotary assets from New River usually spend one to two weeks away from base (*Courtesy Tony Holmes*)

Nicknamed the 'Porcupine', this Gates Learjet 35 is one of 15 operated by American company Flight International on electronic countermeasures (ECM) work. Officially termed 'Smart Crow' Learjets, these aircraft are packed with ECM emitters and jammers. The US Navy uses them to train AEGIS cruiser personnel to track targets in an electronically hostile environment. USAF and Air National Guard interceptor units also involve themselves heavily with 'Smart Crows', as do the Dutch Navy. Whilst based at Cecil, this particular 'Porcupine' operated extensively with both light attack and ASW squadrons

Right Preparing to pack his gear away into the nose of the Cobra, an HML/A-167 pilot pauses for a moment to think about how he is going to stuff his rather bulging kit bag into the slender fuselage of his helicopter. This particular machine is an AH-1T, a rapidly disappearing mark of Cobra in the Corps as most units are re-equipping with the deadlier AH-1W SuperCobra. Eventually the captain stowed his gear, and still had room left for his gunner (*Courtesy Tony Holmes*)

Alongside the 'heavy metal' assets of Light Attack Wing One (LAW-1), several T-34C Mentors also grace the Cecil ramp with their elegant lines. Painted up in a distinctly non-standard scheme, these machines are used as spotter aircraft for A-7 and F/A-18 crews dropping 25 lb practice bombs on various ranges close to the base. The front seat is usually occupied by an instructor from VFA-106, or a qualified pilot from the frontline squadron whose aircraft are involved in the mission. Besides this task, the Mentors act as LAW-1 hacks, pilots attached to desk jobs within the wing staff taking the aircraft aloft a few times a month to keep their flying skills up to scratch

Left As at virtually all US Navy and Air Force bases the world over, a strong arrestor cable stretches across the runway ready for use in an emergency. There was no need for it on this occasion however as a glossy VFC-12 A-4F Skyhawk gently rolls down the tarmac after a routine recovery

Below Another device found at all naval air stations is the Fresnel lens system, or just simply the meatball. This innocuous looking device can make or break a naval aviator, his safe arrival on a pitching carrier deck at night relying solely on this piece of kit. All approaches at naval air stations are flown as if the pilot was recovering on a carrier, the squadron landing signals officer (LSO) regularly heading out to the LSO shack to grade landings

Orion

Below Representing the ultimate naval air ASW platform, the Lockheed P-3 Orion is an aircraft abundant in numbers in the Jacksonville locale. Taxiing out to commence a long Atlantic patrol, this particular Orion is a P-3C Update III machine, the most advanced spec currently available to frontline squadrons. As with all US Navy units operating the Orion, this particular squadron has deleted any distinguishing markings from the aircraft's fin and fuselage, thus rendering individual identification virtually impossible

Right Caught just as the pilot cleans up after take-off, a blotchy P-3C Update III climbs out from NAS Jacksonville. The elegant lines of the Lockheed L-188 Electra clearly show through in today's Orion, the basic airframe remaining the same externally as the less than successful airliner it was developed from. The Electra was Lockheed's first post-war commercial airliner, and was aimed specifically at short to medium range routes. It first took to the air in June 1955, claiming the distinction of being the only American airliner to enter service powered by turboprop engines in the process. A victim of the jet age, production of the Electra ceased in 1960. The two number modex sprayed onto the forward gear bay door is the only form of identification left on frontline P-3s

High above the clouds, the flight engineer monitors the engine instrumentation as his mount drones on out towards the patrol area. From his vantage point, the engineer has a commanding view over the cockpit instrumentation, as well as the ocean down below. A typical Orion crew will include two engineers within its ten man complement

Overleaf The heart of Orion, the ASQ-114 general purpose digital computer linked with the AYA-8 data processing display system. The various ASW systems mounted within the P-3's fuselage are manned by five highly trained crewmen, these TACCOs (Tactical Co-ordinators) tracking and plotting acoustic returns on the brand new IBM Proteus processor. The majority of the Orion fleet is equipped with the less advanced AQA-7 DIFAR (directional acoustic frequency analysis and recording) sonobuoy set, but all new build Update IIIs have Proteus as standard equipment

Above The small overall wingspan of the P-3 in relation to its fuselage length has always been a distinguishing feature of the Lockheed product. Immediately aft of the wing root, within the red rectangular box, are the sonobuoy chutes. The buoys are ejected from the aircraft with explosive cartridge actuating devices (CAD), eliminating the need for a pneumatic system as fitted to earlier Orions, and other ASW aircraft. A total of 87 sonobuoys can be carried by the P-3, these consisting of both passive and active devices

Opposite above The US Navy has a total of four patrol wings in frontline service, three of these being based within America. Consisting of six VP squadrons, plus a non-deployable training unit, Patrol Wing 11 controls all frontline Orion assets at Jacksonville. The majority of the VPs use the baseline P-3C model Orion, but VP-16 operate the Update II version. The training unit, VP-30, operates all versions of the P-3, thus giving them rather more aircraft than the usual nine-Orion complement which makes up a typical frontline squadron. This aerial view of NAS Jacksonville shows just a small part of the seemingly endless ramp which is covered in Orions

Opposite below Carved out of the lush Florida vegetation, NAS Jacksonville is not too far away from the lovely city itself. Besides being the home of frontline and reserve Orion units, Navy Jax also houses the P-3 rework facility for the east coast. Total airframe refurbishment can be achieved at the facility, a tired and high-time Orion entering the hangar at one end and emerging months later in full Update III spec wearing the latest in TPS colours. In the foreground of this view a long line of tiny ant-like sailors carefully walk down the P-3 ramp looking for FOD (Foreign Object Debris), the bane of any aircraft engine

Above The neat mounting of the Allison T56-A-14 turboprop onto the low thin wing was so successfully accomplished by Lockheed back in the 1950s that the P-3's replacement, the P-7, will use a virtually identical arrangement when it enters service in the mid 1990s. The T56 is one of the most reliable engines ever built and provides the pilot of the aircraft with enough power to safely fly it with only two engines in operation. Many patrols are often flown with one prop feathered to extend the over water time available to the crew

Left A line up of suitably immaculate, factory fresh Update III P-3C Orions bask in the warm Florida sun. Housed in the long slender boom is the ASA-64 magnetic anomaly detector, or simply MAD. This device looks for blips in the earth's magnetic surface, these blips being caused by a concentration of metal, which, the Orion crew hopes, is in the shape of a submarine. When in operation the boom is extended aft to increase its effective search radius

Above A VP 'groundie' carefully slots a sonobuoy into one of the ejector chutes. The buoys can be loaded externally on the ground before the sortie commences, or by the crew during the mission. This allows the tactical navigator to choose his acoustic spread depending on the situation at hand. The price of active and passive buoys varies according to their sophistication, but conservatively they are valued at about $5000 US each, give or take a few $100

Right Sandwiched between two conventionally camouflaged P-3s, a low viz cousin is prepared before departing on a patrol. New build Orions are still entering service in the 'old' grey and white, but some refurbished airframes are appearing in Canadian style grey

Right Corrosion is an enemy the US Navy is constantly fighting. The Orion spends a lot of its time at low level tracking targets and is regularly doused in seaspray, thus making the aircraft even more susceptible to the problem. As soon as the P-3 recovers back at the air station the pilot taxies it to the huge wash rack to desalinate the airframe, before parking on the squadron ramp. The low viz P-3s cause the maintenance crews even more headaches because the TPS paint is extremely porous and it absorbs a lot of the moisture encountered during sorties

Below The groundcrew of this P-3 have certainly sweated buckets achieving the gleaming finish on this immaculate machine. The small pod fitted beneath the port wing root contains an ALQ-78 ESM (electronic surveillance measures) passive receiver which listens out for, and identifies, radar emissions. The new P-7 is to be equipped with wingtip mounted AN/ALR-77 pods, built by Eaton, which will also provide targeting data for the aircraft's Harpoon missiles

About Jax

The imposing structure of the NAS Jacksonville tower. As air station control towers go, the facility at Navy Jax is quite spacious inside, offering the controllers an unobstructed view of the field. Departing from the main strip in the background is a reserve C-9 Skytrain II

Buried within the control tower
structure at Jacksonville is FACSFAC,
(Fleet Area Control and Surveillance
Facility) the operational heart for the
many surface and aerial warfare
ranges off Florida's coast. All users of
the Atlantic ranges are vectored into
and out of the area by sailors working
within this tactically lit centre, the
FACSFAC controllers being
responsible for over 64,000 square
miles of airspace

Above Various training programmes are continually run at the base, some being more practical than theoretical. An example of one of the former, captured here in action, is the 'helo dunker' survival course. Before being allowed to fly operationally in a Sea Knight, Sea King or Seahawk, potential crew members are instructed in the art of survival in case a ditching situation occurs. A large steel barrel, fitted out with a typical helicopter interior, is lowered into a deep tank of water then rotated around until it is inverted. Once upside down, the fully kitted trainees are given the signal to bail out in an orderly fashion, if that is possible when you're standing on your head immersed in a deep pool of water! Fully qualified sailors are on hand should anything go wrong, the shadow of a wetsuit-clad instructor floating ominously in the tank just in front of the dunker

Right Some way from home, a rather dirty VAW-12 E-2C Hawkeye cruises over the threshold on approach to Navy Jax. Performing the function of the Replacement Air Group E-2 squadron for AIRLANT, VAW-12 fly out of NAS Norfolk, Virginia. The filthy appearance of the underwings on this machine indicates that the Allison T56s could be running slightly rich, or perhaps the crew just left the polish and cloths back at Norfolk. VAW-12 machines deploy regularly to NAS Key West to operate with fellow RAG squadron VF-101 'Grim Reapers' in perfecting vectoring techniques for new crews

Opposite above and below Sharing the ramp with the 'flocks' of P-3s at Jacksonville is VR-58, one of two reserve C-9B Skytrain II squadrons in the Navy. Tasked with fleet logistics in support of Atlantic naval assets, the C-9s fly thousands of miles during the course of a year. Based on the DC-9 Series 30, the Skytrain II can carry both passengers and general freight. The original Skytrain was of course the ubiquitous Douglas C-47 (R4D-5), many of which performed sterling service for the US Navy. VR-58's sister squadron, VR-59, are based many miles away at NAS Whidbey Island, Washington State. The only other military user of the C-9B is the Kuwaiti Air Force who operate two DC-9 Series 32 machines

Above The 'amphibious Orion' of 50 years ago, the trusty Consolidated PBY Catalina was arguably the first modern VP aircraft issued to the US Navy. Built in its thousands, the elegant Catalina fought in every theatre of World War 2, and was flown by virtually all of the allied nations. As a tribute to former VP personnel that served at Jacksonville many years ago, and to provide an historic link for new members of the VP community, a preserved PBY-5A Catalina is parked near the base entrance. Although looking a little worse for wear, and liberally covered in guano, the Catalina is periodically removed to a hangar within the base and resprayed

Mayport machines

Above Combining good looks with an extremely effective avionics and weapons suite is an achievement aircraft designers strive for but seldom achieve. However, Sikorsky with their S-70 family of helicopters have produced arguably the most attractive rotary machines currently in military service. Developed to fulfil the US Navy's LAMPS III (Light Airborne Multi-Purpose System) programme, Sikorsky was selected in 1977 to provide the airframe to house IBM's advanced ASW avionics suite, the heart of the SH-60B Seahawk. Now, over a decade later, almost all of the 204 aircraft ordered by the Navy have entered service, this particular machine belonging to HSL-40, AIRLANT's Seahawk training unit

Right Unencumbered by the 'Speed Jeans' of the fast jet community, the Navy helicopter pilot only has to cope with the standard issue life vest. Firmly strapped into the left-hand seat, the co-pilot slips on his gloves. The visibility offered to the crew through the Seahawk's heavily glazed cockpit makes landing on board a pitching flight deck quite a simple task

Above The crew go through their preflights while the 'groundies' stand by for the signal which will tell them that the pilot is ready to fire up the twin General Electric T700s. The high tech blades fitted to the Seahawk are formed around a hollow oval titanium spar filled with Nomex honeycomb material. Using epoxy graphite/glassfibre to form the bulk of the blade itself, Sikorsky claims they are tolerant to 23 mm gunfire damage. The rotor head is a forged titanium single piece affair which requires no lubrication and reduces maintenance by 60 per cent

Opposite above All systems go, engines running and everything working as it should. All that remains is for the wheel chocks to be removed and Seahawk 401 can taxi out to commence the afternoon's sortie. The prominent square pods mounted beneath the Seahawk's nose house Raytheon AN/ALQ-142 ESM sensors, a special crew station within the helicopter being built for the operator of this system

Opposite below The airspace around Mayport can get congested as trainee Seahawk crews build up their hours on type. Besides HSL-40, HSLs-42 and -44 are also home ported at the Florida air stations, these squadrons regularly providing helicopters for the SH-60B detachments operating from the small flightdecks of Atlantic Fleet frigates, destroyers and cruisers

Opposite above Captured on the holding pan just seconds from lift off, this Seahawk carries a brightly coloured Texas Instruments AN/ASQ-81(V)2 MAD basket on its starboard fuselage pylon, this station being especially built for the vital ASW device. The colouring of the MAD is rather incongruous when placed alongside the low viz grey used on the rest of the helicopter

Opposite below Both airborne aspects of battle group protection meet briefly on the Mayport taxiways. Whereas the Tomcat is charged with defending surface vessels from aerial attack, the Seahawk is responsible for dealing with the sub surface threat. Transitting from Oceana to Key West, a VF-101 'Grim Reapers' F-14A rolls out to the main runway to continue its journey. Meanwhile, an HSL-40 Seahawk departs terra firma on a training sortie. Rest assured that the red building on the right of the photo is not the Mayport control tower

Above With the pattern now clear of stray fast jets two HSL-40 Seahawks depart on a joint sortie. The prominent circular bulge immediately beneath the cockpit houses the Texas Instruments AN/APS-124 search radar, a powerful system built especially for the LAMPS III helicopter

Opposite above Flying over typical Florida swampland, this Seahawk crew would rarely operate over a similar landscape during an Atlantic cruise. Besides providing the fleet with ASW cover, HSL units also undertake hazardous search and rescue (SAR) missions in times of conflict. During the Persian Gulf operations in 1987 Seahawks flew patrols armed with .50 calibre machine guns and 7.62 mm miniguns firmly mounted within their cabins. There were no reports of these weapons being fired in anger however

Opposite below Mission accomplished, an HSL-40 machine flies over the squadron pan on its approach back to Mayport. The Seahawk has an excellent communications system which enables it to operate closely with its mother ship, or any other vessels which can interface with its Sierra Research AN/ARQ-44 data link

Above Following the estuary back towards base, a well-worn SH-60B cruises along at about 1500 feet. The trusty T700s which power the Seahawk have been a success story for manufacturer General Electric. Selected in 1971 as the powerplant for the US Army's utility tactical transport aircraft system (UTTAS) helicopter, which evolved into the Black Hawk, the first engine was test flown in February 1973. The turboshaft engine also powers the AH-64A Apache, the SH-2G Seasprite and the AH-1W SuperCobra, the T700-GE-401 being the special navalised version fitted to the SH-60B

Above The pilot carefully taxies his mount back to its parking spot on the ramp after completing another training sortie. Like other naval aviators, a Seahawk crew will spend approximately six months with the training squadron before being posted to a frontline unit

Left Several dark green UH-60s break up the monotony of light navy grey at Mayport in the form of 'stealth' Black Hawks. Operated by the US Customs Service, they are used extensively to combat drug trafficking into Florida. The Black Hawks come from US Army stocks and have special infrared seekers and high powered searchlights fitted to them. Although flown by customs officers, the UH-60s are maintained by naval personnel

Besides being home to Maritime Patrol Wing 11, NAS Jacksonville also hosts several SH-3H Sea King units, one of them being HS-7 'Shamrocks'. The 'Shamrocks' are usually attached to Air Wing Three aboard USS *John F Kennedy* (CV-67), and have the dubious distinction of being one of the first squadrons in the Navy to low viz their venerable Sea Kings. The aircrew do, however, still emblazon their bone domes with the fighting green shamrock. The ubiquitous Sea King will still be in frontline service at the end of the decade, but its replacement, the SH-60F Ocean Hawk, is now reaching fleet squadrons on the Pacific coast. A new training facility at NAS North Island, California, has been specifically constructed to ease the type's transition into squadron service, the west coast RAG, HS-10, being charged with the responsibility of running the Ocean Hawk course

Opposite Like the sprawling facility at NAS North Island in southern California, Mayport is also a home port for two fleet aircraft carriers. Both are veterans of many years steaming across the globe, and are actually sister ships. Looking more like a floating slab of freeway during rush hour than a modern fighting vessel, USS *Saratoga* (CV-60) is seen carefully docking back at Mayport after an extensive 15-month refit at the naval dockyards in Norfolk, Virginia. The 700 plus cars parked on her flight deck belong to members of the crew, the Navy transporting them down from Virginia to Florida free of charge. As is common practice when a naval vessel enters port, the ship's company surround the edge of the deck dressed in their best summer whites. Air Wing 17, headquartered at nearby NAS Cecil Field, call the 'Super Sara' home during Atlantic cruises

Left The main runway at Mayport is visible in the background as the *Saratoga* is edged ever closer to the wharfside. Moored behind is the veteran USS *Forrestal* (CV-59), the name ship of this class of vessel, and also the first of the US Navy's super carriers. Having seen over 30 years service since commissioning, the *Forrestal* usually deploys with Air Wing Six aboard. Both carriers have undergone extensive refits in the last three years and are now virtually as good as new

The weekend warriors

Not exactly naval aircraft, but the F-16As of the 125th Fighter Interceptor Group (FIG) are based at Jacksonville International Airport. A fighter unit with a long and proud history, the 125th traded in their elegant F-106 Delta Darts for the far more nimble Fighting Falcon in 1988. Part of the Florida Air National Guard, the 125th are the favoured adversaries of the F/A-18 student pilots assigned to VFA-106

Left 'Check six matey!'

Above Sticking close to his leader, the wingman, with the author aboard, keeps station in his F-16B during a tight climbing turn. The lead Fighting Falcon carries the standard centreline tank which is cleared for most F-16 tactical manoeuvres

All the 125th's F-16s are Block 80 and 81 aircraft and have seen extensive service with frontline units before arriving at Jacksonville. However, their age is not physically apparent in these shots, the line chiefs taking pride in their aircraft. When first delivered the Fighting Falcons wore a dark blue band on their fins upon which the famous lightning bolt was emblazoned. However, the blue has since given way to a more tactical shade of grey. The squadron can trace its ancestry back to the 352nd Fighter Squadron, a unit assigned to the Eighth Air Force in Britain. Flying P-47s and P-51s from June 1943 through to VE-Day, the unit earned itself a formidable reputation in battle before being temporarily deactivated in autumn 1945. It was reformed in February 1947 as a unit of the Florida ANG and equipped with the F-51D. The F-80 Shooting Star soon replaced the venerable Mustang, but was in turn superseded by the F-84E Thunderjet, an aircraft the 125th saw combat in over North Korea. Returning to Florida in late 1952, the unit was briefly equipped with a whole host of assorted machinery ranging from the weary Mustang through to the F-86A, F-80C, T-6, T-33, C-45 and the trusty old C-47. Reaching group status in 1956, the unit has been part of the Air Defense Command ever since. The squadron has progressively operated the F-86D and L model Sabres from August 1956 to June 1959; the Convair F-102 Delta Dagger from July 1960 to autumn 1974; and the F-106 Delta Dart from 1974 to summer 1988

Right Even in the inverted position our trusty leader maintains his station. Spatial disorientation can easily occur when flying tight ACM manoeuvres on a clear blue Florida day over the crystalline waters of the Atlantic

Above Returning to base after the sortie illustrated over the previous pages, the ANG boys fly a neat four-ship line astern before breaking and recovering at Jacksonville. The odd bod out to the left is deliberately holding his position away from the formation as the man occupying the back seat is none other than your intrepid author

Above With years of experience between them, flying a neat four-ship formation like this one becomes second nature for Guard pilots. The beautifully balanced planform of the General Dynamics fighter can be appreciated from this elevated view. Unusually the weapons fit on the lead two F-16s differs from that on the trailing aircraft, only one AIM-9L apiece being mounted on their starboard wingtips

Opposite above Expressing 'Southern hospitality' in a slightly different form, a Tennessee ANG KC-135E from the 151st Air Refueling Squadron tanks several 159th F-16s. Based at McGhee Tyson Airport in Knoxville, the 151st is the second youngest Guard squadron in existence, and a former fighter unit that operated F-86s, F-104s and F-102s throughout the late 1950s and early 1960s. Things got a little slower in 1964 when the beautiful KC-97 Stratofreighter began to replace the sleek F-102 on the McGhee Tyson pan. Eventually the elder statesman of the Boeing family was replaced by the newer KC-135E in July 1976, a move that coincided with its reassignment from TAC to SAC

Opposite below Having returned from the photo sortie, the pilot taxies the F-16B back to the hard stand, the 'groundie' out in front signalling that all is as it should be after the landing

Mission accomplished, the weekend warrior 'de-planes' within the sheltered protection of the 125th hangar bay. Because of the squadron's close proximity to Cuba, and the frequency of Soviet surveillance flights straying into the ADIZ (Air Defence Identification Zone), the 125th maintain a three-minute alert status for a trio of fully armed F-16As, the pilots regularly rotating through this immediate readiness state